Radical Normalisation

Celia A Sorhaindo was born in the Commonwealth of Dominica. She migrated with her family to England in 1976, when she was eight years old, returning home in 2005. Her poems have been published in *Verse Daily*, *Illuminations International Magazine*, *Rattle*, *Mslexia*, *Wasafiri*, *Anomaly*, *Magma Poetry*, *Lolwe*, *New Daughters of Africa Anthology*, and Caribbean journals *PREE*, *The Caribbean Writer*, *BIM*, *Moko Magazine* and *Susumba's Book Bag*. She is co-compiler of *Home Again: Stories of Migration and Return*, published by Papillote Press and her first poetry chapbook, *Guabancex*, longlisted for the 2021 OCM Bocas Prize for Caribbean Literature, was published in February 2020, also by Papillote Press. Celia is a Cropper Foundation Creative Writers Workshop fellow and a Callaloo Creative Writing Workshop fellow.

T0020998

Radical Normalisation

Celia A Sorhaindo

CARCANET POETRY

First published in Great Britain in 2022 by
Carcanet
Alliance House, 30 Cross Street
Manchester, M2 7AQ
www.carcanet.co.uk

Text copyright © Celia A Sorhaindo 2022

The right of Celia A Sorhaindo to be identified as the author
of this work has been asserted in accordance with the Copyright,
Designs and Patents Act of 1988; all rights reserved.

A CIP catalogue record for this book is
available from the British Library.

ISBN   978 1 80017 239 5

Book design by Andrew Latimer
Printed in Great Britain by SRP Ltd, Exeter, Devon

The publisher acknowledges financial
assistance from Arts Council England.

Contents

This book is dedicated, first and foremost, to the loving memory of my father, Martin Clive Sorhaindo. Also, to 'mad' and 'messy' people, past, present and future; those 'locked in attics' real or imagined; the disbelieved; the shrew, 'wandering womb' women; those deemed to be too sensitive, too loud, too wild; those who see the world in a flood of (dis)ordered symbols; those too far away from 'normal'... in-sane... out-of-their-right-minds; those who toppled or were tipped over the edge by this beautiful, but complex and often pain-full, existence on earth. And, to those understanding healers and helpers like C.G. Jung, Malidoma Patrice Somé, R.D. Laing and Dr. Gabor Maté, to name just a few; all our wise, 'medicine' men and women, our shamans, prophets, gurus; all who are effectively using and developing compassionate, balanced, holistic approaches to help fractured souls heal themselves back to a home of wholeness.

Finally, to Vievee Francis, who helped me understand what a radical, revolutionary and necessary act 'being yourself' truly is, and from whom I first heard the phrase 'Radical Normativity'; and to the work of Dr. Charlie Heriot-Maitland, that I came across online soon after, in one of life's serendipitous moments, and his phrase 'Radical Normalisation'.

Poetic Turn Of Events

Today, The People are giving back,
mirroring, throwing light, honest
feedback to The Poets; uncovering
cryptic metaphors; deciphering line
breaks; telling The Poets exactly what
they feel-think of them & their loopy
poetic turns; in plain old unrhythmic
language; in no uncertain terms. It is
quite a revolutionary sight to behold &
The Poets do not know what to make
of it at all, at all, at all! The People are
asking The Poets to listen; hear & read
them for a change. I know! Crazy, right?
What point is The World turning to?

Survival Tips

When they start to shout at us
after saying come talk, trust us
this is a safe space,
tell us this is for our own damn
good little girls
little boys
but our guts
tell us this feels
bad
kicks and warns us
they are trying to ram
shame or guilt into our mouths
trying to hurt us
or stockholm-syndrome smiles,
sparkles in eyes, confuse and dazzle us
Think—
we have been here before
Think—
they are not our star gods,
Think—
they are not
our father
or mother
Think—
even if,
we are no longer children,
Think fast;
should we prise fingers from throat
of our opinion
run run run
or fight

this time
or
be still—

decide
to do

nothing
because
we trust
even though we don't know we know...

Bibia be ye ye (everything will be alright)
—Twi saying

All shall be well, and all shall be well, and
all manner of thing shall be well
—Lady Julian of Norwich

Dead Poets, Prophets and Bob Marley

What if we dare
to be
seen?
: Pushed silently
screaming, writing or singing,
torched under magnifying glass in sun.

We'd rather play behind the scenes,
before curtain is raised.

Better to bury our heads in black sand,
whisper love poems to crabs, than be burnt
or murdered like witches and warlocks
by our own
sparks of ardent action.

What if we dare
to be
heard?
: Given enough air
waves for poetry and reggae strong
and true enough to free—words to hang on.

We armour ourselves with silence
and we're sure it will protect us.

Better to bury our heads in cloud porn,
clasp hands over mouths like mystic
apes, than be garrotted with our own
chain of thought—crowned
with lyrical thorns

Haruspication

this poem born before Sin, Moon, on the edge
of void; before thought, after thought, beyond
end of time elastic, the elemental conundrum;

began as chthonic seed rooted in cavernous
mind, with crow caw, whale call, time chiming
celestial cymbals; single cells raptured in duet;

began with imprecations; began
beyond belief, the pagan stardust
nature of no-thing and every-thing.

This poem born blue, woad or lapis lazuli
crushed into Jean-Rhys-lily-livered black
blood; born blue, blue, indigo star sky blue;

Abani, Walcott, Caoimhín High Mas
blues—a long time, old time, brown D-
flat blown in and out of obsidian rage.

This poem: began heavy, thick-
knuckled lump on throat
kick in the belly button;

began light, striped cheshire cat sits on heaving
chest, not-all-there   or all here, hypnotic
golden eyes, mouth crescent mooning;

began in vice of voice
silenced; in acts of sedition; in truth
and lie solomon-knotting tumours;

began in falling in, falling deep-dive-
down in like aliCe; in phosphorous self
possession; in defiant self

defence. This origin blue print, carbon
copy poem, was dammed to the point
of spilling out rebillious guts

it did not know it had. You
divine reader see

what you and I find in the still
warm entrails of this poem.

Tension Created in Genesis Genius

Start where we all remember
—Glyn Maxwell, *On Poetry*

The signs are all there,
I imagine I have sunk
to the infamous bottom
of this bleak blank page

enveloped
by negative   space
black death in
white air

dark mood
light life
marbled in
white-hole doubt,

unable to turn heart, head
or hands to anything positive.

[Breathe out]
[Breathe in]

Ahh, but I re-member now…amid the dazzling
disaster of school daze—shame-filled, pleated
skirt, blouse and bird-brain Breeze-washed days
—that first scared day—I was taught

chirography at convent preparatory
school and had learned to speak and read
a little before that—a few symbol-ic spells
conjured with nothing, the matter with me;

so though this history has us staggering,
has proved to be rumpled and ragged,
some ciphers can at least be written
out, spoken out, cuneiformed out

naked
even
neat—

black marks bulleted
all over
white space.

Once upon a time
you and I will
rest—part the well red
reeds—balance fonio grain of
truth between

       black   and   white

lines.

Let me reverse the arrow of time, reflect, unwind,
turn my chicken licken feet, knobbled head,
knocked by pitted pinecone-shaped coconut,
and unravel this skein scribbled skin of me.

Oh god, sister, brother, which
moons suns heavens this time
will fall when we start to tug,
hold on to loosed golden threads…

Look at me! Thrice great
Thoth flip-flop feet flipping
backwards, starting at the bottom
of this rim lit black page.

In the beginning was the word
Ancestors called him;
(Ra
or ever living.)
In the beginning
ancestors called him (Amen-Ra
ever living; everything
you say, so be it.)
—Julius S. Lewis, *The Old Tambou*

Crucible

I don't know why she likes this hike so much. She's always been a weird one; loopy
stamina for nature for sure. This is my first time and already it feels like
one time too many. Me, I prefer easy predictable, a steady stable flat
line existence. A guide with some tourists gets a kick out of spinning
stories about the people who never made it; fell off the edge, broke
bones, or got lost and were never seen again. For sure, this ain't no
delicate Disney destination for those who want things real safe
and clean; this is the real deal real. Lord, this rainforest track
is every boring shade of green and this muddy slope has my
feet weighed down and slow. I have slipped, fallen on my
arse twice so far, and I dare not think what break-neck
depth the tall grass at the edge of this dicey mountain
track is hiding. I would turn around now if I wasn't
so scared to go back on my own. She keeps pointing
things out. Tells me look. Listen. Constantly stops
to appreciate the clear sky view. I do not want to break
head-down steady steps to smell no flowers, look up at
no trees, spot no elusive birds. Just want to get there
and back in one piece. Tick that box. Been there, did that!
I'll even buy a tacky t-shirt if they have one. We trek
through the Valley of Desolation and I think any
minute I'm going to crash into the centre of the earth
and ignite instantly to ash. Steam and water woosh up
through cracks in sulphur-yellowed, thin crust lunar surface.
The landscape is extreme; either drenched or parched. Colours
sombre or surreal. How does anything survive here, let alone
thrive? I stay close to her, follow her lead. She has hiked this
trail so many times. I have no idea why. My lungs and feet
are swollen, breath quick and short. In fact everything feels

soaked, moisture filled, but I am cracked-lip thirsty. I am tired,
dead tired and my legs shaky and unstable. I just want to give up
but she says it's not far now. It is a relentless hike up and down
mountain ridges and valleys. After our three hour plus pilgrimage,
we have reached the Boiling Lake just in time to see mist mess
up the view. I scowl. Sulk, is this it? My glasses are steamed up
so now everything is blurred. My copper and silver jewellery
tarnished from the atmosphere. We stand at the edge of the
weather beaten plateau and look down into the ferociously
bubbling water, waiting for the haze to clear. My vertigo is
kicking in and I picture myself dramatically diving into
this natural cauldron. Beaming she says, isn't this amazing.
I just stare at her, frown and sit down. All I can think about,
is that we have to go back the same wretched way we came,
up and down. I start to feel a little better sitting still here
on this piece of terra firma for a while, catching my breath,
but then wonder how much soil the elements have eroded
underneath us over time. I remove my glasses, wipe them
clear. All of a sudden I see a million sparkling particles
dancing in a trick of light. A wow escapes. But just as quick,
the changing sun or cloud or tilt of head, makes the golden
motes vanish. I try to refocus; searchlight bright vapoured
space in front my eyes for what I pray I will see again.

In The Air

After the hurricane,
my grandmother,
in her basement storeroom,
hunkered down,
knelt
her knees raw with prayer
the whole long long lashing tail of night, then
ascended slippery stairs
hoping by holy intervention
her home had been saved.
She stared from room to room,
swaying like a punched drunk spirit,
mouth and eyes wide black holes of disbelief,
words gone as wounds appeared.
She walked on water,
treading over eighty years of floating debris,
then could do no more than silently thank
her saviour over and over for sparing her life.

After the hurricane,
after Mass,
tales of rampant looting
circled among them like hungry dogs;
after the turned-inside-out but still well
clothed congregation, still
silent, had shared signs of peace.
No one appeared to conjure and divide
loaves and fishes between some people;
divided by good and bad luck or circumstance;
divided by ability or will to pad and prepare,
concrete seal, pantry stock, insure against calamity.

But having enough or not enough saved,
surely meant little then,
after all none were saved
from that almighty
hurricane that reined in our poor
island and had everyone drowning.

After the hurricane,
came the crazed lines for food…
for any kind of fuel;
came the tell-tail spoors
of rats and roaches tracking rubbish;
dank despair
threading desperation through the dark.
At night my grandmother floated
in and out of light, nightmare-laden, sleep,
waiting for the chain rattle
of locked door;
for the bark signalling predators
had come for what little she had left.
She prayed for enough strength and grace
to give the strangers what they came to take.

After the hurricane,
she said sometimes it felt
like man eat man survival,
every woman for herself.
Who had time, air, breath, breadth enough,
to free dive deep and long enough,
to understand
then these heads heaped,
backs breaking,
carrying stolen mud-crusted sofas, sinks,
spirits,

through debris to homes
miraculously still standing?
To understand then the tragic
improvised or organised
bacchanal trashing of schools and stores?
Who could explain anything then?
Understand or explain anything now!

When she was able,
my grandmother told me
about after the hurricane.
Months later I flew home
and stood stone still
in the ruin of her home,
alone.
I thought
fear
faith,
had been uncovered,
illuminated, as I watched
a mass of untethered particles
air-floating in the beam of
my head
lamp, from floor all the way above
my head
to the star spored heavens.

Hypotonic

not one of us understood
how the water got into the
sealed places that she did;
the unopened containers—
shut drawers, the basement,
the closed-up vessels—we
cried and cried for months—
even now writing, I well up.

H2.5AZ (Strong Ties, Galvanized)

They are building me a new roof since the old one went
with the wind—category 5 +. I have learnt a whole new
vocabulary—purlins, rafters, wall plates, hurricane ties.
It is chaos on top of chaos—the necessary brutal breaking
down to build back better, stronger—mitigate against future

blows they say will come more frequently—ferociously unpredictable.
I look up—sturdy wet new treated pine above my head, see the thicker
rafters—bird beaked—sitting tied down on edge of anchored plate.
They say you must have such cuts and ties to firmly lodge onto ledges—
the price to be secure—to be more—permanent; more knowledgeable?

Disturbed

Back home red-mad blue-sad from a day of un-healthy close queues and tense un-natural masked quiet in the un-settled city sweat drenched and dead tired I shed clothes shower then systematically retrace all touched surfaces and spray them with alcohol like some thorough stealth-thief.

Cracked phone on silent I slink off into back garden bypass wife's sacred special space lay alone on shaded ground put rough hard hands over ears obliterate all sound I don't want to hear or be here or communicate with anyone don't want to commune with nature's incessant chirpy chattering.
…

Stress.
      Stress.
            Stressed.
                  D i s t r e s s e d
                       tight chest
Cardiac arrest?
Rest rest   rest   REST
Me, a wound-up and worried mess.
…

What? Me? Scared?
Deep slow—hell no!
Not. At. All.

I never. ever. thought
I'd live
to see god
all-mighty chaos… again.

I never. ever. thought
the world would turn again
cryptic and apocalyptic
so. damn. soon.

[shrug]
There's nothing
normal.
That's all

Knock On Wood

Awake early, for a change, I shake my husband
to tell him my dream; my dead dad had said,
we need a place to rest and chat in the garden.
8 bricks, 2 wood-planks later—ta-da!
A bench knocked-up from bits of Mum's
hurricaned home. The fence repairs to keep
the neighbour's male, kale-addicted goat out
would have to wait. We made the seat together.
To sit in heat and breathe humid air.
A new health ritual to join the herbal teas and exercise.

We decide on basic rules. No virus or apocalyptic talk.
There is enough fact and theoretic noise around
these topics already. No human sound at all is fine.
Together 30 years we know to listen for when
one of us wants to be, comfortably, or uncomfortably,
silent. We're alert to nature's quiet too; ears fine-tuned
for warning changes in environmental chatter.
He slowly grinds some home-grown,
self-roasted, coffee beans and I grin
to myself, knowing how this goes.

He will 10-minute-time the gas-stove pot
for its drawn-out brew, and I will stretch an extra 10
for richer flavour. We take our mugs out.
Mine hand-painted, rim-chipped but treasured;
his, plain cream and logo-stamped from Starbucks.
We walk barefoot through damp grass and I try
not to trample the tiny mushrooms I notice
for the first time. I wonder if that fungi
film I watched last night on YouTube brought them
into view. I tell my husband how minute

mycelium, intricate under-our-feet fibres,
communicate; sole connects us
to under-ground worlds. How they are
our ancestors. He sceptically smiles. He turns
to show me the trees, miraculously thriving still
since the hurricane; the thick row of sugarcane;
the hollow where the mango had been ready to gift us
its first fruit; the steady hum of bees bee-ing all over
the little lime and large moringa blossoms—
an awesome sight and sound we feared

would not return. Yesterday, my husband chopped
off rotten cherry tree branches, after one fell heavy,
bang on his head. We laugh about this
precarious life we've survived thus far;
each scared, scarred, sacred point, leading to this
conversation, over this coffee, on this bench, in this
garden, in this country, in these times, after that storm.
Entrenched in challenges, we try to imagine
what normal could possibly look like. We rap
knuckles on our wooden bench.

black dot at 3am

along the staircase
        the books are neatly shelved
                in alphabet order.
                        no dust has settled.
the wood steps are wide, sheened, grain
        emphasised with light
                pine varnish. when you can't
                        full moon sleep, you sit here, pluck
a book out of its place; open; read
        whatever you want
                into words.

crafted with care gifts, bright
        dot between books; rainbow colours
                curve the grain of a chunk of reclaimed wood;
                        a green and yellow, wind blowing palm, painted on
a piece of sleek bamboo; two wound-up
        copper wire figures sit silent on a flat, flecked, sea-
                smoothed stone; one has a miniature book, in looped
                        hands, the other, a tiny halo over head.
a pair of brass lizards gaze into
        each other's black void eyes.

there are music instruments,
        quiet now, waiting to vibrate, play
                some unique sound; a newly goat-skinned djembe;
                        a red|green|gold coconut shakshak; a small slim metal
glockenspiel; carved calabash gourd holding
        still seeds.
                out of black
                    grout, the fragment

tile face of a woman emerges; glazed eyes stare; red cracked
        lips turn up a smile; cheeks chipped blush beige, highlight
                base brown. in the bathroom, another mosaic woman walks
                        naked into fractured blue-white sea.

from the top step the cement gargoyle watches; sitting
        sentient on haunches, hands on chin, tips
            of taloned feet touching.
                    you feel the energetic surviving spirits
of hand made creations,
        commune and celebrate this hour
            of life. you alone, see
                  deep down into pale blue dot
eye, of an enamel fish;
        swimming close
            to the edge
        of a sparkling
glass vase; filled infinite
with grains of golden sand.

ten years since it came
everyone has moved on now
but you are stuck here

storm naming season
what can be held which stays still
unchanged tomorrow

june is still too soon
september is remember
unhinged ghosts remain

ground

grinding coffee beans in manual burr grinder on the shimmering front porch. hard to have imagined this roasting bright blue day, glaring after endless weeks of rain and grotty smoke-grey skies. it is a slow blissfull ritual. measure out dark brown arabica. carefully fill slim metal well. just look at these beans. every single smooth curved body, split down the middle like miniature brains. turn the handle clockwise. each round a rhythmic pleasure sound and feel. grind. grind. grind. bottom pilling high with mass of broken bean grounds; a necessary grinding down to release *french roast* flavour. intense and smoky. when the tension goes slack, know it is done and fill the shiny stainless-steel pot. inside dark stained over time. wait for the bubbling, then turn heat to slow simmer. wait specific stretch of time for required strength. add sugar and savour. in these minutes let mind turn herself over—grind down broken times.

Deep Mined

I hate telling my wife about any new
song I like. I know she will play it to
death. I think about this while washing
my hair. How her mind is uncomfortably
inclined to deep-mine whatever it makes
contact with. I don't know why, this trait,
threading through-out our years, annoys
me so much. I hate how she sucks blood
marrow out of bone too; how she stares
down dark brink's edge. I read the sham-
poo bottle. An obsessive habit of hers.
In black ink it says rinse out thoroughly.
Then, I read, avoid all contact with eyes.

(T)Here...Like...

The purpled heart still pumping its bloody way round.

The tatty hand-stitched quilt spread tight and tucked under corners.

The thin slippers shoved under the bed each night.

The bag that holds and carries, then lays folded in some dark space.

The dust settled unseen somewhere, untouched for years.

The dripping shower cap. The damp towel drying on the rail.

The soil in the garden growing grass, weeds—flowers that fade.

The unmoving face of the kitchen clock still on the wall.

The unread books. The boxed tissues.

The current concealed behind concrete, behind sockets, in wires.

The useful used things put away in drawers—left hanging in cupboards.

The mirror; lake; tarnished silver spoon; clear window after midnight.

A hurt-too-much splinter underfoot, you cannot take out;

a back; shoulder; thimble; physical photo album; turning loose ring.

A cliché.

How each and every time you turn

around and look in their direction, they never turn

and look, nor

walk, away—not ever

doh let me be lonely

…good, good night. kekeke. mi jus rememba readin wah de
wise man say in mi son cleva people book oui, *the snake which
cannot cast its skin has to die.* maybe dat man know de secret too.
but mi sure mi know more bout skin an odda tings dan im,
more dan any wizened man. kekeke. son, mi only kin, mi flesh
blood, bone born, where yuh be? mi kill a snake once. true true.
well nah me dyin tonight nah. kekeke. wah time it be? 12am,
mus hurry hurry, gettin late. see how time fly, flies by. ave fi go,
ave fi go. kekeke. if dey ketch me dey skin me alive. kekeke.
son, son, why yuh stay away so long? mi feel a dark hollow
in mi insides an around mi outside head. an empty empty.
dey come steal mi tings. mi cyah find anyting since yuh leff.
dey say i is mad. dey say i smell bad. dey say i black black an
ugly, eighty years an more ugly as sin. mi still high backside,
broad wide lips, pain-pivot hips, hung pointed breasts. hagged.
dread-full. dey wan de land. but wah land mi possess? dey wan
disappear me. dey wan mi ard wuk likkle likkle money. but mi
hide it good. kekeke. who dere? who dere? oh oh, winsome
wind, yuh dat dere nah? yuh comin fi ride tonight? kekeke.

son, yuh daddy gone so long long, but mi glad oui…nah!
nah! dat nah true, mi miss im bad bad. his Old Spice close
skin contact. yuh an yuh fadda same same smile like a simile.
kekeke. hurry hurry, mi av fi hurry, but mi bent bones slow,
breakin. who tell me live so long nah? kekeke. nice nice lawless
lifetimes doin wah mi will doh! no-one go tie an wind me
up…but lonely me lonely. always lonely. long time lonely; in
mi blood blue lonely. mi kill a skinny cat once. mammy yuh
happy up dere wid God? mi bet yuh two pally pally. even alive
yuh were already martyr. daddy try hide his breath but we see
signs pon yuh skin, an unda yuh thin skin. kekeke. mi hang it

by it tail an skin it a new way. cleva mi cleva. son, dey stealin all a mi tings. is wicked dey wicked. hurry. where mi mortar nah? where fi hide it tonight? mi rememba dat time policeman john from de village look up at de wrong time an see me. bang bang. mi fallin. mi fallin. mi tinkin life ova fi sure. kekeke. but de old silk cotton tree ketch mi fired tail an hide me good good. son, come home nah. dey comin in mi home an stealin mi tings. doin wah dey waah wid mi in broad broad day light. dey say i deformed.

mi skin. hurry mi ave fi hurry. where fi hide it good good? cyah let dem find it. sprinkle salt. kekeke. tonight dey nah ketch me nah. mista, is yuh mi gettin tonight. mi see de way yuh treat yuh wife. tek her high vitality. nasty yuh nasty. mi comin an fix yuh good good. kekeke. hurry. quick turn in de mirror, last look at skin. look me now! mi a real naked shame less glowin serpent. dey waah mi home, all mi save up an down. ave fi go. wind good good. sky clear, slither moon. mi see nah rain till mornin. mi flyin fast an high, higher dan icarus. mi bright bright, power-full tonight. all mi light life mi fill up wid energy. kekeke. dey tryin ketch me out. which human neva like a witch hunt? dey teasin me, pushin me, callin me names. mi help dem birth dere babies good good. show dem where an how fi bury de coiled silver slither of cord, an why. mi give dem all de knowledge, de right herbs, de bush teas, de hand-down old-time remedies, de spells fi a spell ah fright, fi a turn ah nerves. dey doh even tink fi ask wah hell mi ketch in mi skin dis life, wah mi see, wah mi feel, wah mi know. kekeke. mi nah worry doh. someone ketchin fire tonight. hurry. son mi miss yuh. dey doh even look me in speck ah mi spark-eye. come home nah. mi know de islan small small but it deepa dan yuh tink an de vibration high high. plenty plenty unda de surface. mi ave tings fi show yuh, teach yuh, good good high knowledge, wisdom fi fill yuh up, mek yuh unda-tink ova-stan every tiny tiny ting in de whole universe. mek yuh know yuhself bad bad. good good. mi reach de crossroad. mi land. kekeke. mista gettin a taste tonight. well, mi too gettin a energetic taste oui. kekeke. god, why dey wicked so nah? wah mi do, mek dem treat me like dat? mek de children throw stones, call me names. push me.

hurry. 3am. sun cyah ketch mi tail. keyhole, crack or unda de door tonight? good good, mi nah see nah rice. mi kill a cow once. why mi sense someone watchin me nah? who dere? who dere? kekeke. doh let me ketch yuh nah. yuh smell me? yuh smell mi heat bad, mi bright burnin? mi smell yuh. i'll be good fi yuh. mi comin. comin fi suck yuh. mek a blue-black bruise. mark up yuh neck. wicked yuh wicked. mi mek yuh highjump pale right out ah yuh thick skin. i is eight, an de nun English teacha say is dunce i dunce. point at mi poem spellin. mek mi stan pon table wid a pointed red D hat pon mi head, whole class laughin laughin. but she know me smarter dan her, is shame mi shame her. mi reach. mi comin. kekeke. mi come show yuh de god awe-full fearsome flamboyant hellfire yuh yellin soucouyant. kekeke. kekeke. but mi just pullin yuh big toe. just playin wid yuh. is nah vengeance mi come tek nah. uhuh. look. here. mi leff yuh a morsel ah worm-free immortal glow, someting hidden, fi silver slither slowly coil unda yuh skin. kekeke. let me flee oui. thunda an lightnin. rain comin. need fi fly home quick quick before sun return an turn fast fire pon me. hehehe…good good night.

Forge

Come! Come! Look! See!
We are breaking
the broken people into
good good poets and
it's quite a sight to behold.

A spectacular
public spectacle, poet
herself in crisis,
that just *has* to be seen...Xperienced.

The bright but uptight women, and
naively animate animas,
they especially meltdown best;

excess gas lit they burn blushred then
lightash; smoked out
like saints and la diablesses.
Wow! Look at their fired pirouettes, their
poetic turns no longer cold-contrived.

To be brutal
honest, weren't they pretty damn awful?
Well now they're uncomfortably authentic;
real-pain painted, jagged-jazz musical. Quite
exquisitely vulnerable, don't you think?

Come! Come! Look we need
a thousand witnesses
at least. We are making magic;
awe-some alchemical gold from coal

centres of already beast
beaten people; frictioning
the living dark sparks
right out of them all.

Come! Come! Look! See this
whole-some hardcore foundry sweat
shop work of pathetic poets; perished-
in—now surrendered to real free-
willed venerable potent-
ial; ferociously fireworkedup
and spinning; just burning
to wield role of reel hell

erasure drawn...sketched out

1st scene

the lines i draw out from memory

are what's left; just a few sketchy two-dimensional fragments i do

not trust; they're never the whole curved out picture; but still

etched in the body is what I felt then; feel still

with this recall

—

i know though—thorough tracing

over the original event, would be more

accurate, but who ever has access

to that expansive archival source

—

i sketch out the stripped down

bare bones scene yet again; first

in my head, then

with pencil; graphite lightly dividing

                                                    lines
on landscape turned, rectangled paper
                                                    lines
of trees on the edge. crooked, jagged
                                                    lines
for vine covered branches and leaves…
                                                    lines
for fractal veins, for grey curved clouds
                                                    lines
marking out boundaries where

vehicles should park : the lanes they should drive within

—

a previous Me, the only person here; an older dot I positioned

on curb in-front octagonal stop sign, still, drawn, down…

waiting for green go to cross two wide

deserted lanes—that Me, on this side—

and everyone else on the other—

visibly undrawn—statically silent

guillotine sliced silence(d). dark not golden

—

what

                                                           line

had I crossed, that I could not see then—

still cannot see—

was not even aware existed

what other

                                                           lines

should i draw now; which

                                                           lines

to cross

over or out; rubout; reveal; which

                                                           lines

to stand

behind, within, on or alongside—

with or without permission—

aware of or not

…
exile(d).
exile(d). erase(d).
exile(d). erase(d). left alone.
eXile(d). erase(d). left alone. left Out.

backs turned but no turning back—

although that is where I find myself—

i found Myself—turning time back over and over—

going back, going back over—

re-turning. re-drawing. laying lines of past

on this blank paper space in front of me

fracturing fault lines forming where I stood

—

what remains undrawn

what remains unchanged

what remains mis-understood

unseen. unknown. unknowable.

—

i am no skilled visual artist. too

many things i cannot draw, paint,

realistically re-cap(ture); not

even impressionistically. but

do you see Me in this lined sketch

—

well, i don't want you to

so, I now erase(d). unreal-

istic juvenile lines I pictured

drawn out of memory again

life is never linear... although line-age

surely colours some scenes. plus

silent treatments never truly mean

total silence, do they—communication

lines still remain clear and open—somewhere...

like Pádraig said, in cutting silence i too heard the community

of madness that I am and

i know now, i |belong|be al(one)| here

broken—parsing

line breaks and drawing

reasonable safe faith-

full circles around—i will

not continually loop—wheel my

shaking body back there again—

where I did not belong—

should never have been—

will I

2nd scene

imagine
colonies of
single-celled organisms. algae; fungi; bacteria—
compartmentalisation; separation; survival; life-cycle; self-
assembly—
transformation.
imagine damage-re-pair.
re-member-in

3rd scene

what boundaries separate
in outer space
what lines are drawn between attractin or repellin
atoms and molecules
what is the ultimate separatin line drawn in|across this life form
what inclusive|exclusive clue-less void is left by re-moving
that el line in space

4th scene|seen|seein

it's ti(me) for an(other) virtuall meetin
who is zoomed out
and in and how deep
out or in
should we go

and for how long

just to hear our own
heart beatin sound

and then leave enough space
to hear clear, each other's

i suspect
there are infinite
clearly complex individual
perspex perspectives—
even simply sensational
childlike ones… some drawn
down from a purpled blood-line
invisible but not erased

Stigma(ta)

Primal comfort from picking scabs,
short but sharp and jagged nails
punctuating healing wounds, again.

Triplicate painful pressure
pleasure; high
from finger tip control.

Something else we cannot leave
alone, like mosquito bite itches
and some unwhole men... women too.

Why not point out our st.igme wounds
like signposts, even when self made,
parade them proudly to the world?

SanctifyIn101HeadRooms

Earlier today, I counted, took stock of
the 13 physical homes I've lived in so far.
Hoisted up chest fulls from memory storage;
examined each numbered address:
342a, 74, 286, 35, 11... where are they all now?
And all the experiential feel-ins
their 101 rooms contained? I wonder if
turbulent energy still ghosts old haunts?

But, all ancestral wound
wound-up, life, right in here
is where I was fundamentally
most at home; energetically alive
and safely livin most of the time.

          right here hermetic
   sealed   spaced-out
   intuitive   informed
       compartmentalised

inside my moon-womb head,
within these close quarters;

in this attic.

in this bedroom. in this walk-in clothes closet. in this bathroom.

in this livin room. dinnin room. kitchen. study.

in this cellar.

Multi-cellular mind-
full. Every room with a view
point my own. Bird brain lookin
in, wakin and liftin lids to peek out
at sunlight through bright dot eyes.

Right here, I've wandered,
played and pondered unique
to universal, understood,
chit-chatted, heart-to-hearted,
trained brain, stood ground.

When all hell rained
down, runnin scared,
spineless, me and my body
of selves stayed sheltered
in a-maze-in safe shell.

No! You can never gas
me right out of my light
mind; push and force me
out of my mind over
matter mind; my firm-
ament mind; my body
politic mind. Not for
burnin money or love.

Listen, I will loosen
grip, let go, give up
every material thing;
make myself crazy
to keep hangin
out inside here.

Let's get to the hard heart
beat of this matter. Will-
fully I've looped freewheel-
in self, round and round
about self centred mind.

Marvin, I'm rememberin home
is never where heart, or hat, lay.

Lauryn, I've found in's a way
out of bound boxes and chains.

My universe is mental, I think
so am I. E. E. for God's sake—

this is the only thing that matters
now,
ever
after

thick black
ink
inside
here

I Am Not Amused

Listen! I. Am. So. Freakin. Mad! This bloody
poem just barged its way into my body. Did
not ask me first if I wanted to play host. Did
not ask if it could use the material matter of
my life experience to make its bed and lie
down its mess-age on this clean white page;
bring its wildly re-purposed words to solo pen-
paper party. It makes already hot blood boil over.
Jesus! Who do these poems think they are? God
Almighty? Ancestors? They are not even familiar
family. They just passive-aggressive their thick-
muscle selves all over the universe. Spark-spread
and fire-up their perverse viral verses everywhere.
Freakin narcissistic gas-lighters! Some of them
don't even know yet what it is they want to say,
clearly; have not taken some quiet time-out to
think their feelings through; solitude and reflect;
before crash-coursing into my plane of reality.
Then they blame ME for being born half-formed;
ask ME to clear things up; make them whole or
abort their ugly massed mess; like it is something
I was double-bound born to do. But I have never
killed off an imperfect poem yet. I'm leaving this
freakin mad one right here. You deal with it! You
make sense out of it! Question why it is here, now!

Thalassotherapy

I am outstretched, belly up,
on back, bare, buoyant,
osmosising the quicksilver
body-hugging Atlantic; agitating
waves cooling, calming, cleansing.

These scorching times, hard
dog days, and again I have
melted under glare, judged
too soft, and dread parched
and silenced my only defence.

I cannot say
when this shaming
fear first landed;
a fly, sowing larvae
like infinite seeds.

float—breathe out—breathe in—float

I smile and recall you and me
foraging wild berries in forest.
Pulsed by memories energy,
ablutions drift anxieties out—

You handled the soft fruit so
gently, cradled them back. I was
a silent eight year old, scared
on seeing the worms.

You guided—
showed me how to soak
berries in sink
water with salt—gently agitate;

we watched berries float free
from bloated worms
which drifted out—
dead.

My Sister & I Are Picking Mangoes

again in Mum's debris garden. Our tropical life has been
entropically re-coloured since the hurricane passed. She
came to help us & the hourglass days, turning over & over,
are often sublimely beautiful & surreal; brown pleasuring

to green/yellow/red; starred silver indigo, far too visible.
This beloved mango tree is recovery; she has us in awe
with her constant, almost embarrassing, fruit full giving.
I hold my husband's green fishing net: I know what it's

like to fall, bruise, split skin & expose flesh all the way
down to bone-white seed, so I pull down & catch; save
some mangoes from this fate. I imagine though the fruit
innately sense my nonsense; knowing there is no sin in

falling—grow, fall, feed ground/gut, grow again, repeat
infinitely. Brown hands pick up any spoilt grounded fruit,
throw them in the grown green gutter. Our aim? Deter flies
hovering around; seeding worms unseen into ripening fruit.

Mary Wollst.onecraft Shelley and I

At the point of beginning there is
always the Thought, the Imagined
moon lit Sin-full Word—she created
hers Monst.er a creature like me? ta-da!
look how easy we birth carbon copy
monsters like Gods. I think a marked
beast can sometimes be a St.

Cut(ting) Act(ion)

For and after Shivanee N. Ramlochan

Spirited bard, wiry, pale, was invited home.
Father bowed, honoured by this presence.
We scraped a meagre but honest welcome
together. We put on a show, our offerings.

Young sister lyriced Africa. My coarse hair
raised in time with her fist. But our guest
was not impressed; told us to stop poet-ing;
put the dot of us squarely in our place. Firm

bottoms pinched, we open mouthed, silence,
not knowing what else to do; sat too long
respectful on edge of hard seats. Eyes turned
up to our father, confused, we waited for him

to save us; sat wordless and took poet's point-
ed word splinters; drew them down to bosom.
I did not stand that day; no hand, head, voice
of mine raised to remove the barb; silent—still.

Home was never the same after that. Hung
with shame, stung; we had missed some red
bullseye; judged, black-mark slapped by sharp
haloed guest. Why, I could not understand.

This is what happens when I politely leave
pricks alone; they infect, peck away at flesh
lips; keep me quiet for years. Parents, do sons
and daughters need saving by, or from, poets…

or priests? Which you think still; keep them dead
holy or wholly alive, hopeful? Neither? What use
are musings on muses if not words de-ciphered
by me, us? I'm careful who I'm told to worship

now, just due to some words; I cut the spell words
from the actors who bound them down, then I act.
Look me, trying to stand, speak up now in poems.
Too late you say to hear from poet—father, priest?

Go on, tell me off. Tell me I should hush, flush
my mouth again. Why should I be scared of one
more sacred dead hungry haunted ghost? Chupes!
Shivanee wrote Everyone Knows I Am a Haunting;

no fear, we are all aghast, haunting; bared, barbed—
pointing, appointed. Are you not hating hurting?
Leave me let me seek/speak this ghost; wind it
in, blow it out; serve it up in verse. Welcome,
                    welcome—
                                        well come!

Like Paper Cuts...Like Being Cut Up...Like Paper

In the poetry workshop we are discussing

similes and I'm struggling with the exercise.

What is a paper cut like? My brain frantically

roots round for things to pick up and compare.

Finding nothing it scrambles around a bit more—

then—screams back at me, a paper cut is like a

freaking paper cut, for god's sake, why make it

look like something else? There is talk of tenor

and vehicle, but so far, in this class context, to me,

seem nothing like the real things, so become just

more random words to learn, remember, carry around;

in case they may be useful later. I push past my brain,

search my memory my self. paper cut, paper cut...

Do you remember the unexpected stings from thin

veiled slights, off-hand but serrated comments—

that deeply tore you up inside? Such insignificant

little incidents, no one that important—but so thin

skinned then, they hurt like hell. Funny now, looking

down at scars…1,024 shallow wounds so easily open up

on this once blank page—paper cutting me over again.

Lying In Own Unmade Bed

moon light	dark night
bed time	bad time
unmade	unmade
blanket	blame
cream sheet	defeat
tucked in	undone
purple fleece	in pieces
valance frill	crushed still
quilt	guilt
hand-made	made mad
patchwork	worked up
cover up	cover up
snuggle up	stitched-up
soft pillow	hard pill
silk cushion	suicidal
fluffed up	fucked up
sturdy	disturbed
stable	unstable
strong frame	spineless
firm slats	slated
head board	head butted
pine	pain
wood grain	drained
put together	dismantled
well-built	brutal breaking
patted down	punched
hot water bottle	throttle
frame mounted	mount defence
warm	worn out
comfort	confront
pleasure	high pressure

mosquito net	death threat
protector	projector
pocket sprung	hung up
memory foam	deep depression
firm mattress	matter of fact
new	who knew
lying down	damn lies
tired	tired
lights off	suicide thoughts
meditate	medicate
good night	fight or flight
lay still	do nothing
sleep on back	face up
asleep	waking nightmare
slumber	pulled under
dream	scream
snore	can't ignore
nice sleep	narcissist
well rested	well tested
deep sleep	death wish
awake	woken
calm	karma
get up	stand up
bed made	make amends

animula : rapture of an Introverted Narcissist

Death must not find us thinking that we die
—Martin Carter

*

little   me
*

past life   has shamed   me
current life   is shattering   me
I keep losing   my self
        i keep finding   my self
I keep   u n r a v e l l i n g
*

who made me
        irrevocably singular never plural
who made me
        immutable pronoun never verb
what if you
        cut me in pieces consume me
what if you
        freeze me evaporate me
what if
        demented brain fractures leaves body alone
what if
        only memories magic mythical me
what if i
        alter my core change given names
what if i
        shed skins find I wasn't there
do I
        die return pick up where i left try again
do i
        live different fractal in infinite realms

*

I keep losing   my self
      i keep finding   my self
I keep   u n r a v e l l i n g

shamed shattering   a future i saved
*

I forget   to remember
    who made me
    what if
    do i
i remember   to forget
*

shamed. shattered. bein
    no doubt saved
        i'm river yieldin to
        see: numinous   neurons
                mirror   project
                me   you
                in everyone   everyone in
                you   me
        see: divein   behind why
we will kiss our eyes blind

[Breathe out]
[Breathe in]

no   matter
I
never just   matter
we
always   matter
we make it all

```
                     matter
—once—
there was
no                   matter
yes                  matter
was                  im-material
```

---

it is of prophecy.
how one dies
as a series
of questions
and resurrects
themselves
to answer
them all
—Gabriel Ramirez, *Dove With Hooves*

Hintergedanken

For and after Paule Marshall 09.04.1929 – 12.08.2019 (RIPE)

I was the only real thing on the planet that day   I
cuckooed out; the unleashed salivating dog of my
rational mind off somewhere, playing hide and seek.

It was inevitable, I guess—you know
only too well what I mean, although now
may not be the time to remember.

Ancestors—who else to blame—heirloomed me to a US state, a hotel
lobby crime scene in the south. Dissolved, like poetry I loosened ugly
sepia blood stained into velvet cushions, short tasselled like telomeres.

Don't ask me why they led me there. Perhaps to feel,
betray(ed), unearth buried bones, to testify, to hurt, to hurt, to   hurt...
Who knows? Maybe to libate a water-wine miracle.

After all, if I remember honestly—strike
that—no memory is the whole truth so   help me
god—from what hindsight allows me to recall,

there was a wedding celebration in progress;
glistening light skins and dark skins, a frenzy
of circling shark white teeth, bright brown eyes.

Then that Tinkerbell flash, like switching
off an old TV set, or a minute atomic flare...after,
I was care free, fearlessly flying with fairies for weeks...

But like I say, never trust
dreams, confabulations—true or false, I am led
to believe whatever I am ready to—

but remembrance—ah Paule
remembrance...all the timeless,
the chosen, people and places...

Vodou

Now—
if I stick these pins

at pulse points beneath skin—for every sorry
sorry I've silently searched for from you—

you too—I can make of myself a pretty
gruesome voodoo doll—cushion myself.

Watch me—here again at 3am—wailing
moon witching hour hanging over all

these glistening silver pins
I have gathered.

—Listen—

I'll take this sharp pain—
I'll stash away these pins—

I'll be—
Sorry!

Joining Dots is Radically Normal

Clear a universal
space, I feel
I am coming
apart again—

this mind has become
unhinged enough
times now to stop being
concerned:

Me, no different to the mad
woman I saw working
the join-the-dots book using
her own rules—Shaw's black

girl in search of Ahmunic God?
—inking the sur-real visionary
symbols she needed
to be guided by.

Me, all totems and talismans
training mind to open, mouth
to close at will; all effort after meaning
to magic my future ancestral gods;

joining dots like the ones we
are taught to look up to,
Orion's waist belted ant tight with
imaginary lines—words between legs.

Me, honestly, just another
straightforward poet, spun by eMotional turns
of tide-changing moon
and shadowing sun;

joining dots—dropping an embarrassment
of atomic words; effecting internal
revolutions; creating myself naked
revelations—or is this poet

just madly pulling
together previously perfected
pieces, an internet age Saint
Isidore. Being disciplined

in this craft is extra
ordinary; super, natural,
like linked Ouija board
hands tracing invisible
lines drawn before dawn.

What You Propose I Do

I really don't know about evil
   enough; its primal primeval
      genesis; lived experience of
         vile villainous Eve or Devil;
            tempted seeds; deeds unseen.
         Proposition 64 says knowledge
   of evil is inadequate knowledge.
How to know which is the lesser
of two to follow? Who proposes
   the parts which will will dispose?
      I imagine some one can turn light
         on what tap tap taps the dark root
            shadow; what will prevail overall;
         illuminate darkside moon/money.
   Jung I hear unveils answers to Job;
   I haven't seen them yet. You know
your view on this? Can you relate?
   Vices firmly grip all my five senses.
      If desire is source, what shall I make
         of hunger to pull de-tail; devour evil?

B for Bravo; Bravo for Bee—
A Musical Language in B♭ or A#

For and after Kei Miller

My 50th year finds me fleshing out Bony chicken wings
out of this Body. People this age should pick choice Bones
with you, I hear all over social media; By this point they've
mayBe lost some Bite reflex. I try to Bury Bones, But end
up mining the decayed like a demented dog. I have enough
collected Bones now of my own; teeth too, to gnaw them
down still. Lately I've Been feeling a heated fusing of B-
ones. The mirror shows a knoB-Bled spine has full grown
Behind my Back. I see a serpents jointed tail and fine fore-
limBs primeval and evolving. Been winging it, all this time.

*
* *

Hear this—that Bone Body Buzzing B flat; A sharp music
riff-ting, ting ting; that necessary tense chord. I am no
thing But lashing Breaking wing Beat on surface—Bee.

listen

After Damian 'Jr Gong' Marley

you speak life?
speak only when told to?
never say what you want to?
they can trap you
bind and warp you
can use all against you
both silence and words too

still

learn to speak life
articulate as you do
you can switch and snitch too
word how you need to
love hurt if you want to
know words can see through you
speak life recreate you

listen

so speak life
Damian we hear you
even if words double-bind you
can tongue-tie you
they can free you
just say what you have to
your silence won't save you

you speak life?
can we even hear you?
when you speak the unsayable?
silence can speak life too

listen

Fragments of Epic Memory

For and after Edward Kamau Brathwaite 11.05.1930—04.02.2020 (RIPE)
and Derek Walcott 23.01.1930—17.03.2017 (RIPE)

Chupes! I see talk continues still about the way we sound:
standard english, pidgin, nation language, dialect, accent,
mellifluous patois. I don't know where the noises I make,
fit, in any of it. No clue which side to take. Dominica born
but Ipswich raised, my husband says on the phone, I sound
so strangely Scottish, and if I try to patois or dialect with this
accent…well…let's just say, it sounding funny funny oui :-).

Yesterday I saw a headline on social media, World's languages
traced back to single African mother tongue. It was a US academic's
'Laughable!!!' comment, that baited me click and read. I also learned
dolphins click communicate their seen images to each other. Today, I'm
reading The Secret History. A machine with metal parts is sliding in
and out. Forming images. An Inca temple…click click click…Pyramids
…the Parthenon, and these words push a piece of magic forward:

a while back I fell. Hit my head hard. Just a hairline crack the
doctor said; no dizzying spells; no black-outs; no noticeable
memory loss; no loss of speech; no need for concern; but for
months after, quiet click click clicks were added to my internal
dialogue. Weird, but not worrying, I thought then. Now, I think,
perhaps history's phenomenal fragments still lie low; beneath
Breath, Eyes, Memory; constantly changing every moment;
affecting each phoneme we make up, sound out, inside or out.

Brain Damage Control

Hmmm…perhaps it was not a great idea to push headlong
out of Winkler's Lunatic straight onto stratum path of Okri's
Famished Road. We all know some books & lyrical hooks
can have your hard & hairy or soft jelly coconut heads split &
spilling—opened; have you wondering just where your brain
thinks it's wandering too—all on its own—no lead from you.

I was just thinking what a cool superpower; to communicate
with trees & bushes, Germans too, like Aloysius, Jamaican
madman of 1,000 names… I swear one of his names was Bay-
gon—don't worry—it's a Caribbean thing, like Crix, crackers.
But seriously, mind-tripping with spirited Azaro; winds blowing
spells over sea, riddling sand, vortex voices & lapis lazuli chants.

Pink Floyd now, not my drawn colour, but their words are in
no way nice or pretty. If you've loonied the dark side of the
moon, Bob Marley wailered good on grass, you may know
what I mean; the sky is certainly not blue, the grass hardly
ever green nor chain linked with white daisies. Star eyes on
black sky face, new moon smile—feel the worlds they shoot.

EHS Prima Materia—Sugoi 69

A high school teacher once asked us to pay attention to our
obsessions. That time I was firm fixed with what stained
the armpit of his white white shirt a luminous yellow;
the benzene ring, the colourless odourless vitriol of H2SO4,
numbers, words, the periodic table, entropy, the heart…
of things…well, actually of me. Trust me,
I have catalogued countless more since.

Ever exploded your head?
Ever broken right down
to your particular particle matter-
ing parts? Turned outside in, down-
side up? It doesn't matter how,
what went wrong. What matters
is what you thought was the cause

of order to chaos; what you imagine(d)
the source to be; the matter with(in) you.

I wonder, was anything altered when you began
to re-member; when you put back
together again sum of your fractious parts?
Point of view (POV) perhaps?

Maybe you started seeing and reading things differently, enquiring.
Drilling in to why you notice the bathroom bottles have been background
whispering all this time. They say White Rain, That's the secret of VO5
or It's all happening on the High Ridge 06905. You see whole words
anagrammed into sword pieces; rearrange to realise, release po-tent power.
Your US spell checker red lines UK spell-ins; s's hiss it warns should be

sleepy z's; U has been removed and u wonder what power games are
played with spellbinding changes. You break everything down, in and
around, you, even and odd words; re-create; re-search. Eyes see y ants
dot their self-determined way through the land of us giants; Isis
hidden deep in blue pi ripple of Mississippi; love loci coiled in-
t(w)o wolves, vowels, clover; hues of man; I See artIStic re-creational
heart of earth, UFO (Unidentifiable [insert applicable F word here] Object).

Look at iron-ic me; Fe(male);
male with a little iron inserted, periodically?
Yup, I have been tabulated/tied-up
in straight orderly columns, so why not
position myself in one more. At least the Period-
ic Table gives objects lettered symbols,
with measurable elemental atomic weight.
I am always converting my name to a number,
to suss if my mind-full self has mass. Sometimes
I turn a little green-grey for my house-and-two-kids,
great job, twin brother, wormed into this world named
William…and I imagine with enough will, i am
anything I want to be too. See how nAme slips
us through a mirror; spills me down
a rabbit hole. Kamau, are we Strange Fruit? I wonder
if we can ever find, liberate, understand
again, any native words our own. This pentagram name
owns me for now; metaphor character
contains a self made home. Anyway, dam right if you
think I'm mad, why shouldn't I be?

And what's with all these :-)? Each way
I turn, Smile Please. O I see what you're
saying Jean, I hear. All Σ'd up—Awe full
evolution, ulti-mate love passion potion!

Bi-polar : Submers-ion...Sublimat+ion...Precipitat(ion)

...this island, atlas water in air, heavy, whirlpooling; washing sweet
salt words. Cup it up to overflowing, drink A to Z; swallow

words from all kinda worlds, spat, whispered; sounded out
by all manna of people. What do you make of that: these

infinitely somersaulting sounds, collapsed in finite alphabetic point;
this mix of dark and light matter words? What do you make of
this gulp of life: where we mete out, heat, eat, devour words like

alphabet soup; where I sip on I love you's in one breath
in, then gurgle out, if you come near me again I will wolf

you down? Anger? Wounded? Ablutions. Atlantic born words
whorling inside and outside famished bi-polar world—vaporising...

Un-Set Binary Bits—Lingua Franca

j says:
i see in the air
god
(not lamb of but Iambe evoL)
in the mirror do not doubt me
i am no monster
am i understood
jung please tell them
i have lost
nothing
in my mind i have
collected streams of infinite
unconsciousnesses
don't know where
to store them
they split my spirit
let me speak
let me put them down here
let me be light
let there be light
which phi-
losophi.cal poet said that
fiat was a method
of transportation transmutation

j says:
charles says radical normalisation
empathic black/white/colourless
ra-in-bow
lead for all growin glowin
misinnerstood
growlin pit bull terrors
tragic poets
artistic creators neurotic creatures
savage body eaters
no need to beware
of the cynanthropic dogs
they do not scare
away the speckled yellow birds
who
let the firemouthed
domini-canis
out anyway
tobenottobe
Iamhere
iamnowhere
iam$\sqrt{-1}$
nofeartime
fornewkoines

j says:
mr bast fate stole your umbrella
pull yourself together
man it was only howards end not
the end of the world perhaps
the beginning remember
only connect
i lost mine today mind
can read too much
into these things
vincent stop screaming the horror
into my left ear torturing
yourself/myself
listen
we are all carrying crosses
opening veins bleeding
hearts
kurtz you are not the only one
control and conduct yourself
you/we crucify/forge our own
selves
fuck fear
hoarding mythical father
let us look at him more closely
maneater? dog/god head
canis baal? vampire?

j says:
consumed consumer take
eat drink drink drink
th-is is his fish body that is is her
blue blood is (s)he dead
yet never my image or imagined
archetypal her(o)
but not guilty perhaps
herodotus is appropriate
oops sorry for the complex
freudian slips
another selfhater or selfæta
he thought
this was where it all began
—child—
that man was so sirius
all pent-up split
sex and mother wound aggression
never live laugh love
where is my mother
(Ye)maya poor mother
—brothers sisters—
why does she/they
always hide her
power
why leave
the men al-one

j says:
he is she is
scared hates/loves
brother/sister
mother/father
…self
g says:
do not be afraid
—child—
love self first
my will will
all ways be done
j says: whowhatwhere is the trinity though in truth
g: j breath let go trying so hard to overstand
unravel your sacred Beautiful Mind
you are a qu-
rious bit of
soucouyant-fire
who chars/lightens
all eyes sparkle
you are
never ever
put out
you are
elemental torrential
hEart & bRAIN.

j says:
hmm hocus-pocus focus focus focus
tune in like ein(st)ein
you know take time e=mc2 can go
both ways when 0I0 φ 101 seen sees seer seed sown
ask simple questions google it or guess
when you break them down
answers always are optional bits
of unSettled binary bible stories bind
back to live/die by a Set
of undecided 0's/1's wavering
no fixed coincidence of opposites
to be not to be
no room for mistranslations
here else permit yourself to write
your translated truth in marginalia
free of shame and stone of madness

Exorcise

Out of blue spectered
Light
Appeared at 3am Dont know from where why
Dark ran Clang to the cobwebbed corners
Honey why you dont come
Into this [guilt quilt] space I opened up
Climb in-through-out this deepred
Heart fiercefired earth
Underneath
Its thicktrickyteethed tucked up layers
You thought
You knew
Me
Me Too
Early bells clanged loud
Loud tefillin twisting knotting air
Wound up the path forward
AllWays bouldered
Both of us
Future lay down long shadows
Misunderstood Torn
Open Shaken beyond
OurSelves Seven odd milleniaed miles we blew
Blue Never knew what we were
Doing here
In the dark
Now in this quiet quite strange quick honeyed
Light
Us two skins seem curiously stitched

ComfortablyCosy Chimes too
Sound
Feel
Different

Conjunctio

peel your own image from the mirror
—Derek Walcott

The sulphuric alchemical
rain here transforms things:
copper capped church patinated
forest green, mountains to mud,
people to primal pulp,
personalities split.

I observed it with my own orb eyes,
flaming twin abluted in torrent,
all matted hair and mucus; tears,
rivulets bleeding blending like
wet windscreen distortion;
sublimed water-colour.

blinked—
sleight of hand
unseen—

and I
was absolutely
gone.

---

we grow and fuse
we break apart
but
most of all
we are one of the same seed
—Imani (Paula) Sorhaindo, *Pulse Rock*

Katabasis

The last breath deaths of the varied copper
toned leaves, keep being played out in front
of my eyes. Onto grey gravel they free fall or
gracefully somersault; lay still as I run them
over in my failing white vehicle; gears stiff
and difficult to change. A crisp, closed leaf has
been stuck in my broken wiper blade for weeks;
held against spreading arc-cracked windscreen.
I think perhaps I should free it. One day I will
remember before driving off. Descending the
steep hill fast, I sense I am late again but don't
recall what for, yet. Where am I supposed to be
this time? All the green leaves are no-wind still.
When I fly past they don't wave me as usual.
I pray morning's first breath be, a grateful one.

Cento—Digesting Know(the)Ledge

For and after Gregory Pardlo

Lonely hero, zero, conceived by shafts of heat
lightning, secrets in blood's chemical record, for-
ever heart-starved hollow, holds the blues current
like electricity & does not know what is inside
that can't be contained. Fire shut up in bones, she
could only begin to imagine tracing a path back
to a quiet home. Look! How little you give of
your self—how little of yourself has been given.

Blessed now and breaking, wisdom bends light
into the eye like the sun's warmth on the back.
Sound it out silent mouth—Yes, I am hurt! Give
words the bodies you consume; any book will do.
Summon heavens for guidance in deciphering
celestial script: starless night; salt on the breeze.
Discordant emotions toward the mute—sound
it out! Finding power where power isn't given.

*
* *

Jumping often refers to something you'd rather
not get involved in, but can tune form to the em-
anations of this vibrant life; the mosquito tones.
There is but one mask that can still be reached
by tender thought, heated ear inside chest, a call
coming from inside the house; a mirror in an eye.
Hear stone sing chariots come to carry us home;
the world of words beyond the curtain of language.
Zero, hero, born a cipher, a whole ledger, a single
word from you might bring the funhouse down.

Masochists

For and after Jean Rhys 24.08.1890 – 14.05.1979 (RIPE)

like
when
a
fish
hook
fits
into
an
open
eye
once
again
powerless
she
could
not
afford
to
flee
free
what
else
to
do
but
stop
tugging
against
the
barb

let
this
sink
in
she
said
I
learnt
to
love
the
lean
into
perpetual
pain
the
conscious
let
go
how
can
I
afford
not
to
use
run
with
exotic
currency
if
I
will
do

that
there's
no
knowing
what
I
won't
do
if
I
will
it
teary
she
smiled
pleased
he
turned
to
cut
the
line
and
run
but
she
had
already
bit
through
he
felt
a
tug

a
reel
back
in
out
of
the
blue
against
his
will

What Do I Know

Mr Elias John-Baptiste says they sent a biblical
hurricane so he could know God. Says God's eye
stayed above his house. Stared him out for 8 hours
just to make sure he was the right one. And he was.
Says God up lifted him high, boomed in air and brain,

look me, look me in this here whirlwind. I Mosiah
come with countless dead millions to help you out.
They do not know what you are capable of; they do
not know what you are thinking. I know you have
wrought well, wrought well; you are well-wrought and

ready to redeem. Mr John-Baptiste tells me all of this.
His family tells me that since the hurricane, he's lost
connection to what is real. His head is gone they say.
Elias lives only on Nood sea salt popcorn and spring
water. He smiles—smiles all the time; leaves hair dread-

ful long. There's nothing we can do for him but pray,
and give pills if he ever disturbs people too too much.
Mr Elias John-Baptiste tells me his mother lives in the
flooded wine cellar of his ruined home. She's a bright
black octopus. She feeds him a tentacle each day that

grows right back. He tells me our tallest mountain has
a flip-top lid and Cristóbal Colón lives deep deep inside.
Says Colón thinks our Zion is the New Jerusalem they need
and sees the twelve tribes of Israel all here in green Eden.
Mr Elias John-Baptiste asks me if I believe in anything

he says. I shrug. I say *Mr John-Baptiste maybe you're just not crazy about this world anymore; maybe you're mad mad mad about something. But what do I know?* He tells me he's the one God chose to heal the world. I say—*Aren't we all Mr John-Baptiste, aren't we all?*

Mr Elias John-Baptiste says he does not know where on good earth to start; has energetic answers now to every single question; exactly how to save the whole damn thing. Just not where to begin. I can only shrug again. *All I know is God did not start from anywhere.*

LOL (101)

After Gerard Manley Hopkins 28.07.1844 – 08.06.1889 (RIPE)

I think the body knows
When poetry is the only
Pulse left to focus-beat
Its breath upon.

Dread ti...red
     all the time—
Dread ti...red
     of it all, this time—
Dread ti...red
     of all
          that ruined
             run-out time—
Dying to be me : *for that I came*
inscape   *to selve*
     instress.

No
Matter if expected or in-expected
Heart attacked
        Crash;
Before bruise, lump, the persistent
Cough, the ache, the invisible puls-
In pain in the gut or groin—comes
Nous's innate intimate in-tuition.

What body does not know
It was born dying to climb the
Ladder of light—
To know the

Language of light—
Live out loud—
Laugh out light from wOmb-silence?

Mind, the cosmic-mine gap—

Full-feel into Poetry's
           Energetic
                      Tune
                                 In
                      Time
           You too
Will know
           When to
                      Spill
                                 Over
                      Then
           Slip again in-
Two being only One
Black nought source-quiet
Nulled

STasis As Revolutionary HEalin

For Malidoma Patrice Somé 01.30.1956 – 09.12.2021 (RIPE)
healing is a revolutionary stance that you take…

      stayin in bed
a few extra hours
isnt exactly revolutionary.
                        i understand.
wont burn the whole place down.
                setoff the necessary

                                 reset.
but its what i want to do against
whispers outside
and inside   my head.

my husbands phone
is ringin
 somewhere
      inside the house.
      wakeup.
          wakeup.
          there are things
              you need to do
                        right now.

      i hear loud crackles and pops outside.
from the farmers field behind.
          she is preparin the land for plantin.
          clearin with a fire
              i hope is under
                  her control.

some smoke wisps into the bedroom.
      air carryin
           the burnin.

     i turn over into a death
pose.
pull covers over heart.
      over my mouth nose ears
      over my eyes.
      over. my. head.
          hands rest crossed over
          chest.
             still.
                 unmovein.
             mind is
                 unwindin
             stillin
                 alight
             deep
                 breathin

Acknowledgements

With thanks and deep gratitude to:
My dear family for your love and support—Mum (Alexandra/
Alix), husband Paul, siblings (Kenneth, Carol, Michael,
Auraum Benneurt/Imani)—Aunty Leng for the inspiring
books I've borrowed over the years and your constant support
for the arts, tt for always keeping it real, The Nature Island
Literary Festival (NILF) organising team, chaired by Dr.
Alwin Bully and Dr. Schuyler Esprit (also Create Caribbean
founder and director) and all who contributed and performed
over the years, Polly Pattullo of Papillote Press, Dr. Kimone
Joseph (Head, The University of the West Indies (UWI) Open
Campus Dominica), Raymond Lawrence and Dominica
Division of Culture, faculty and staff of the Department of
Literary, Cultural and Communication Studies, The UWI
St Augustine Campus, Trinidad and Tobago, including
Dr. Maarit Forde and Dr. Muli Amaye, Vievee Francis and
Gregory Pardlo (The Callaloo Creative Writing Workshop)
and the CCWW Chapel Hill 2017 cohort, Dr. Merle Hodge,
Prof. Funso Aiyejina, Dr. Danielle Lyndersay (The Cropper
Foundation Caribbean Writers programme), the Cropper
2016 Balandra group and all the writers who visited, The
Caribbean Writer and Moko magazine families, Andy Caul
(ACalabash), Tracey Guiry and Maggie Sullivan (The Poetry
Archive), Maggie Queeney (The Poetry Foundation Forms
& Features workshops), Jordan Hartt (Kahini.org), David B.
Dacosta (Black Eskimo Podcast), MJ Fièvre (Badass Black
Girl and Miami Book Fair), BOCAS Literary Festival team,
Brooklyn Caribbean Literary Festival team, Dr. Opal Palmer
Adisa, Danielle Boodoo-Fortuné, Kathy Casimir MacLean
(DASSSA), Catherine-Esther Cowie, Mac Donald Dixon,
Joanne C. Hillhouse, Ian Jackson, Oonya Kempadoo, John

Robert Lee, Vladimir Lucien, Shara McCallum, Geoffrey Philp, Shivanee N. Ramlochan, the rest of my poetry writing and reading family, present, past and future, and to the Carcanet team, Michael Schmidt, John McAuliffe, Jazmine Linklater, Becky Scott, Andrew Latimer and Alan Brenik, for all your kindness, care and support.

Many thanks also, to the editors of the following publications where versions of these poems first appeared:

- 'Conjunctio'—a previous version published in *Susumba's Book Bag* online Caribbean Magazine as 'Disappearing Act'. Issue 10, 2018
- 'Cut(ting) Act(ion)'—published in *BIM* online Caribbean Magazine, 2021
- 'doh let me be lonely'—published in *PREE* online Caribbean Magazine, 2021
- 'Knock On Wood'—published in *Wasafiri*, Volume 36 Issue 3, 2021
- 'Survival Tips'—published in *New Daughters of Africa: An International Anthology of Writing by Women of African Descent*, 2019
- to publisher Papillote Press for permission to include the following poems from *Guabancex*, 2020:
  'In The Air', 'Hypotonic', 'H2.5AZ' (Strong Ties, Galvanized), 'My Sister & I Are Picking Mangoes', 'What Do I Know';
- and to Four Way Books and Gregory Pardlo for permission re 'Cento—Digesting Know(the)Ledge', which is comprised of lines (with changes) from Gregory Pardlo's poetry collection *Digest*, (Four Way Books 2014).